BUTTON CRAFTS
FOR ALL AGES

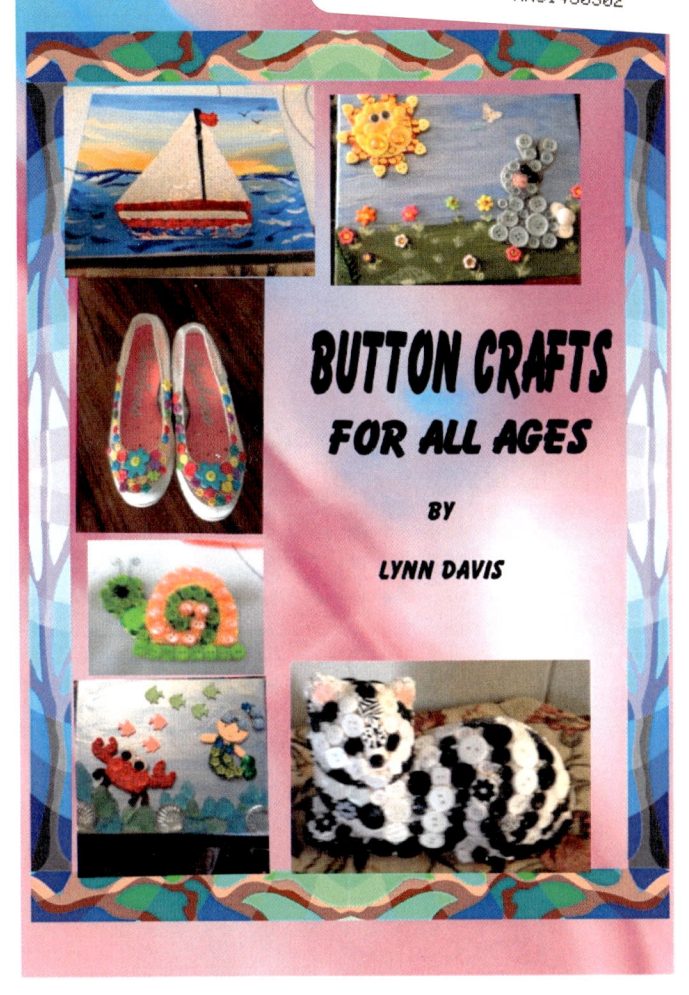

BY

LYNN DAVIS

Buttons have been used for thousands of years. Some are made of wood, plastic, pearls, semi-precious stones and even carved from bone. Buttons have been even used as currency. Even today vintage buttons are collected and worth quite a bit.

When I was younger and my children would come home with a button missing instead of going to the fabric store to try to find replacements, the shirt would go into the bag for Goodwill Thrift store. As my family grew older and times were tight, I learned my lessons and started to replace the missing buttons.

Over the years I would find buttons in the bottom of the washing machine and also at flea markets. There was always some school or craft projects that some of specialty buttons were just perfect for. This book is full of fun projects for all ages.

Mixed Media – some of the projects included will also need the following:

Seed beads – these come in many colors and are great to fill in the spaces between the buttons. Seed beads also are great to highlight areas.

Pictures – some of the project are on canvas or could be on the front of note cards.

Acrylic paints – these paints are easy to use and if you mess up you can just wait until the paint dry then repaint the area. For the projects that are on canvas I painted the backgrounds with acrylics. As an example if you want to paint a sky you can blend the acrylics so that it looks like clouds or even a sunset. To do this make sure your brush is clean and just slightly wet. If you take the brush and draw it across where the two colors it will blend then to look like clouds. I have included a couple of examples in this book for your reference.

Glue

Elmer All Purpose Glue – I used this glue for gluing the buttons and seed beads to wood pre-cut shapes

E6000 Glue – I use this glue when I am making jewelry, great for the metal buttons.

Fabric Glue – clothing projects you can use either fabric glue or hot glue. Rule of thumb is if you need to put the clothing in the washer and dryer use fabric glue. If you are gluing to fabric make sure to put some wax paper under where you are gluing so that the layers don't stick together.

Hot Glue – Hot glue is great for any areas other than fabric.

Tools – Wire Cutters – For cutting the backs of button that are medal or plastic

Shoes

Brown Flats with Pearls Buttons

Items Needed: Flat shoes, Buttons, Fabric Glue

Do you need some shoes to go with that special dress but don't have time to go to the Mall? Add some pearl buttons. For these button use wire cutters to cut off the back where it attaches to the button. Then with some fabric glue the buttons on and you have some nice new shoes.

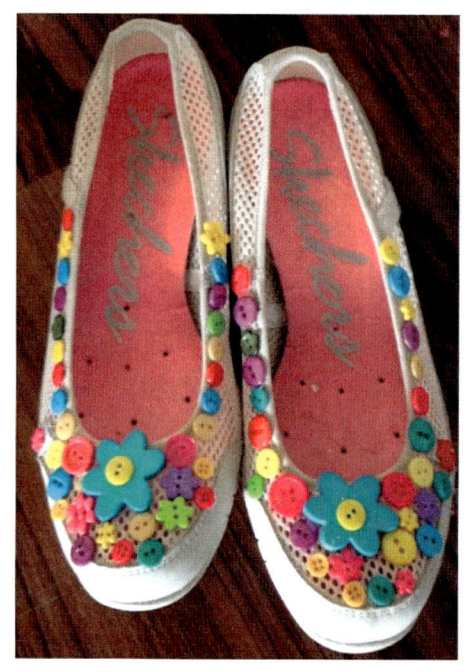

Skechers Shoe Project

Items Needed: Tennis shoes, Buttons, Fabric Glue

You want to give new life to your old tennis shoes? Add some bright color buttons. I found these button on Oriental Trading Company on the internet.

Felt Purse

Items Needed: foam Easter egg, felt bunnies, pink and white buttons, red seed beads, Elmer's clear all purpose glue and hot glue

The felt purse I found at Walmart. The foam egg and felt bunnies I found at Michael's Art and Craft store. The buttons were hot glued on the felt purse. The foam egg was also part of a kit that I glued on the purse. The foam egg already had the cut out design when I bought the purse. I used red seed beads and Elmers glue to fill in the rest of the design on the egg.

Quilted Black Purse

Items Needed: Black Quilted Purse, black and white buttons, fabric glue or hot glue

The quilted purse I found at Hobby Lobby in their craft section. It came complete with the bow. I used some black and white designer buttons I ordered at Oriental Trading. These buttons were plastic so I used hot glue. If you use another type of button other than plastic you may want to check out fabric glue.

Tan Clutch Bag

Items Needed: Tan Clutch Bag, white buttons, yellow/gold gems and fabric glue

The clutch bag I found at the Goodwill Thrift store for $2.00. I added the buttons and gems with fabric glue.

Green Clutch Bag

Items Needed: Nine West Green Clutch Bag, Gold and buttons, yellow/gold gems and fabric glue

This clutch bag I found at the Goodwill Thrift store for $5.00. It was in great shape. I added the buttons and gems with fabric glue.

Snail Button Project

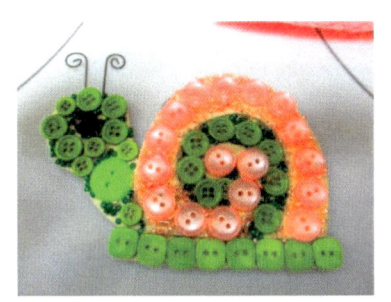

Items Needed:

Wooden precut snail which you can purchase at Michaels
Pink purse I found at the 99 cent store
Pink and green buttons. Green Seed Beads and clear Elmer glue.

This little snail is made of wood. I started with the green buttons which I glued on with clear Elmer's glue. Once that is dry than add the pink buttons. Put a drop of the clear glue in any gaps between the buttons. Once it is completely dry then glue it to the small purse with hot glue. Make sure to put some wax paper inside until the glue is dried.

This only cost $3.00 to make and a great gift for any little girl.

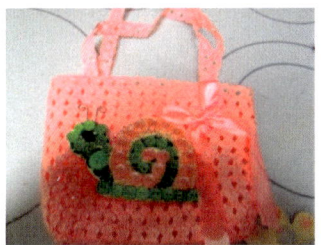

Jean Purse Project

Items Needed:

Foam bunny, felt bunny, vintage girl pin, assorted buttons, gems and glue. I purchase most of the decorations at Michaels The vintage girl pin I found at the Gem and Bead show they have at the Orange County Fair grounds four times a year. Arrange the buttons and decorations out first so that my granddaughter could pick out her favorite.

Use fabric glue to add your personal touches. You can also use Iron-on letters for a name.

SMALL BAGS

Items Needed : Small Cloth Bags, Fabric Paint, buttons, fabric glue

These little bags came in a five pack. I sprayed the bags with fabric dye and let dry. Add some cute little buttons and these are great gift bags.

Half Button Apron

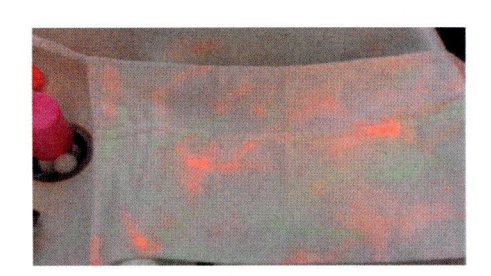

Items Needed: Half Fabric Apron, Fabric spray, buttons and fabric glue

I should have started this project when my granddaughter was selling Girl Scouts cookies. Spray the fabric paint on the apron and let it dry. Glue the buttons with fabric spray or you could sew them on.

You can also use iron-on letters if you want to put the name on the apron,

Fabric spray colors and button Visor

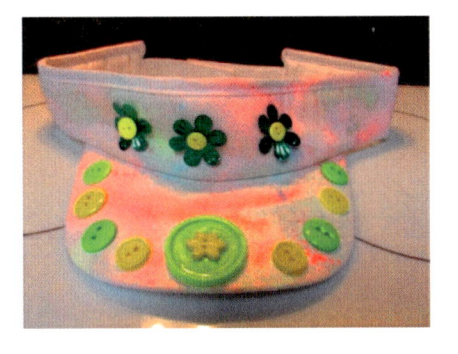

Items Needed : Fabric Visor, Neon Fabric spray colors, buttons and flowers

You can find everything to make this visor at your local craft stores.

Test the fabric paint on a scrap cloth or paper. Make sure to cover the area you will be working on before you try to spray your visor. Let the spray paint dry before you glue on the flowers and buttons.

Headbands

Items Needed: Headbands that are covered with material, buttons, paper roses, gems and feathers, hot glue or fabric glue

These headbands I purchased at Walmart. I glued on the buttons first then added some gems, paper roses and feathers for some fun.

Butterfly Hair Barrettes

Items Needed : Butterfly hair clips and hot glue

I found these butterfly hair clips at the clearance bin at JoAnn Fabric and Crafts. I used a drop of hot glue attach seach button.

If you don't have JoAnn in your area you can make your own. You could use felt, material or even cardboard for the butterfly. You can use any type of material if you put fabric stiffener. Once the material dries cut out the shape of a butterfly and attached the metal clip on the underside and glue buttons on top.

Ski Headbands

Items Needed : Headbands, buttons, fabric glue

At the end of the ski season they put all of headbands on sale. These were only $0.50 each. The first one I found some old pearls buttons. The second I used found an octopus button and two other matching. The last is decorated with a foam bear and six blue buttons.

Valentine Heart Project

Items Needed: Valentine kit, clear Elmer's glue, acrylic red paint.

The kit has everything to make a special heart for your Valentine. The only thing you will need is Elmer clear glue. I found the kit at JoAnn's Arts and Crafts.

Owl Journel

Items Needed: Precut wood owl, journal, clear Elmer's glue, hot glue, seed beads

To start lay out the beads on the wood owl cut out. I do this to all of my project to make sure I have enough buttons. Remove the buttons and spread out the Elmer's glue and start adding them on. Let this completely dry I can use this little owl for all type of projects. My grandson likes to draw so when I found the journal on sale I know this would be perfect for this little owl.

You can add letters on the journal. This owl can be used as a refrigerator magnet, add it to a frame or add ribbon to make it an ornament.

My Journal and Pictures

Items Needed: Precut paper flowers, journal, buttons, hot glue,

This binder is a pre-teen version of a day planner. It had pages for favorite things, friends, drawing areas, etc. I found this one at Michaels. Decorating the front with paper flowers and buttons.

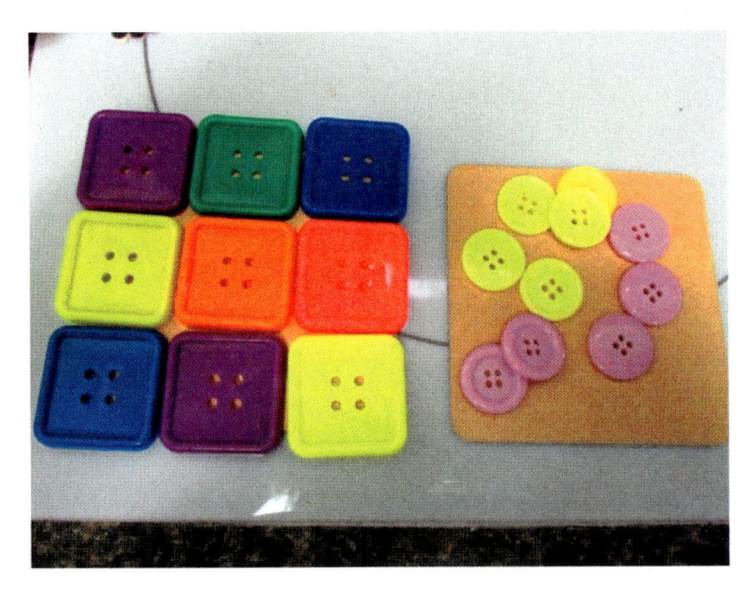

TIC TAC TOE BUTTON COASTER

Items Needed : Extra large buttons, heavy cardboard coaster blanks or cork, 5 buttons of different colors, Hot Glue.

Did you ever go to Cracker Barrel for breakfast? They always had little wooden games on each table for the kids to play with while waiting for their food. I had a four pack of coasters when the idea came to me. Just glue extra large square buttons to the coasters. I tested it on my grand kids and they loved it.

WHALE TAIL PAPER WEIGHT

Items Needed : Whale tail paper weight, white buttons, seed beads and tiny pearls.

This was a challenge because of the curves. Hot glue the buttons first. After this is completed start with small sections and apply clear glue and add the seed beads and pearls. Once that is dry work on the next section and continue until the entire tail is covered.

Pink Bird Project

Items Needed:

Precut wood bird, light pink and heart buttons, pink seed beads and Elmer clear glue.

Arrange all of the buttons on the wooden bird. I started with the light pink buttons then the wing since it is slightly elevated. Once dry I added the bright pink heart buttons for the wing, tail and beak.

You can use this to decorate anything with from gift boxes, as an ornament or glue a magnet on the back so that you can put it on your refrigerator.

Flower Button Hanger

Items Needed - Flower hanger, buttons, seed beads, hot glue and Elmer's clear glue

Recycle old hanger with some peach buttons. Hot glue buttons on flowers and leaves. For the spaces between the leaves use Elmer's glue and seed beads to fill in the gaps.

3D Button Bunny

Items Needed:
Cardboard Bunny, Elmers Glue Clear Colored Buttons of various sizes

For this project I painted the bunny first and let it dry. Next you can start adding on the buttons. There will be gaps which you can add seed beads to cover it. The bunny above is with the seed beads. The back of the bunny is without the seed beads. You can make it either way.

Button Kitten Project

Items Needed: Creamic Cat, Black and White buttons, white seed beads, hot glue, Elmer's clear glue.

This unfinished ceramic kitten was a challenge with all of the curves. I hot glued the buttons first then filled in the gaps between the button with seed beads.

Masquerade Cat

Items Needed - I found the little gold cat statue at Hobby Lobby, buttons, seed beads, hot glue and Elmer's clear glue.

This is the same process as before, starting first the large buttons hot gluing them to the cat. I found some antique buttons for the eyes and the ear buttons was in a package of Halloween buttons.

Items Needed:

Canvas for your painting. acrylic paint blue, white, yellow, black, and orange and hot glue.

When painting the background you will need to layer the colors. I start with blue for the top and bottom. I add orange and yellow in the middle. Clear your paint brush and take some thinned out white and start going between the colors so blend the colors. The nice thing about acrylic paints is that they blend well and if you don't like the out come once the canvas is dry you can paint over it.

To finish this you will need to hot glue the sailboat on with hot glue. Then you can put in the finishing touches by adding some dark streaks for the waves and some birds on the top.

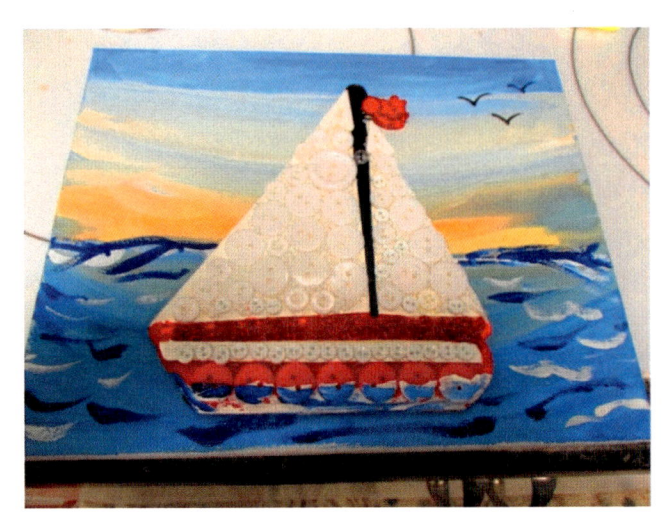

Items Needed:

Precut wood sail boat, light red, black and white buttons, red and white seed beads and Elmer clear glue, hot glue.

Sail Boat - This project has two different parts, the first is the actual sail boat and the second is the picture of the sunset and water on canvas. For the sail boat you will need to paint the sailboat and let it dry. Once dry you will need to add your buttons. For the buttons I hot glue the larger buttons first. You can see the gaps between the buttons which you will need to fill on with seed beads.

Mermaid Picture

Items Needed: Canvas, blue acrylic paint, white pearl paint, glass shells, sea glass, crab and mermaid precut wood, foam fish and lots of buttons

Step One: You will need to paint the canvas first. I used a light blue acrylic paint.for the first and when it is still wet add some white pearl paint. With a wet brush blend the two colors then put it aside to dry.

Mermaid Picture Part 2

Step 2 - Crab - hot glue the red and black buttons. I used medium wiggly eyes. Use red seed beads in between the buttons.

Mermaid - Hot glue buttons first and then fill in gaps with seed beads to fill in.

Assemble the final picture - Add the sea glass on the bottom, hot glue in place along with the crab and mermaid. To finish this I found some foam fish to complete this picture.

Dinosaur Picture - Buttons, Paint and Shells

Items Needed : Acrylic paint, canvas, paint brushes, shells, some silk plants, hot glue

Painting - This painting is just like the sailboat picture. Start with the background blending layers for the sunset and water. Add in the mountains and palm trees.

The dinosaur is a precut wood that I found at Michaels. You will need to paint the dinosaur then glue on the buttons. For the spaces where there are gaps between buttons, I used clear glue and seed beads.

Once the canvas is completely dry you can add the dinosaur and the plants and shells.

Halloween Black Cat Picture - Buttons, Canvas, Paint and plants

Items Needed : Acrylic paint, canvas, paint brushes, shells, some silk plants, hot glue

Painting - This painting is just like the sailboat picture. Start with the background blending layers starting at purple, then blend in orange and white for the sky. The base is green.

The black cat is a precut wood. You will need to paint the cat then glue on the buttons. For the spaces where there are gaps between buttons, use clear glue and seed beads.

Once the canvas is completely dry you can add the cat and some leaves for the tree, old branches and some Halloween pumpkin and spider buttons.

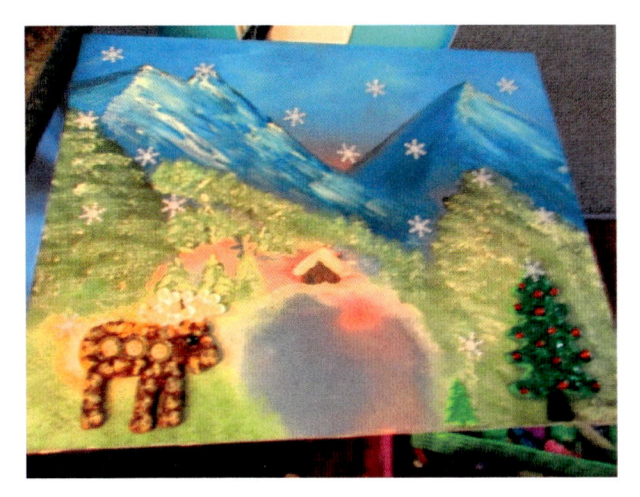

MOOSE PICTURE

Items Needed : Moose and tree wooden cut outs, canvas, acrylic paint, beads and glitter

Part one - background painting on canvas - Start with the sky there is just a hint of a sunrise showing between mountains. You will want to blend the sky with clean brush and water. Mountains are also using the blue but use a little white snow and blend the colors to bring out the ridge line and valleys. Add the green trees, little house and lake.

The moose and Christmas tree are wood cut outs covered in buttons and seed beads.

Bunny Picture

Items Needed - Canvas, wooden cut outs of sun and bunny, buttons and colored gems.

This is the same process as the mermaid picture. Start with the canvas with layering colors and let dry. Next hot glue the buttons on the sun and bunny. Fill in gaps with seed beads. You can add some gems to the sun. The flowers are hot glued and added to the gems in the center of the flowers.

Book Markers

Items Needed: Foam Popsciles , buttons, hot glue,

These are a cute projects for kids. All you need is a drop of glue and they are perfect for any book.

Plastic Race Car Eggs

Use a plastic egg, buttons for wheels. You can cut the opening with finger nail scissors. Use hot glue to put them together and these little cars will be the hit of your Easter Egg Hunt

Mother's Day Flower Project

Items Needed Flower and base and hot glue

I found this flower and base at the Dollar Store. The base was dirty so I repainted it and added some matching buttons. This is a very cute gift for Mom. There are all type of projects you can find there for just $1.00

Mother's Day Mirror

Items Needed : Mirror buttons, gems and hot glue

I found this mirror the Dollar Store. With just some cute buttons and gems this is a very cute gift for Mom. There are all type of projects you can find there for just $1.00

3D Autumn Button Tree

Items Needed: 3D wood tree kit (Hobby Lobby), buttons, seed beads, brown paint, Elmers glue and Hot glue.

The kit is in three pieces to make the tree. Paint the tree before adding the buttons. I picked fall colors for this project but you could do any season. After the buttons are added fill in the gaps with seed beads.

Tree Kit I found at Hobby Lobby

View from the top

SPIDER GLASSES AND MUG

Items Needed : Glasses, mug, buttons, wiggly eyes, hot glue, sharpie marker

These will brighten up any Halloween party. Add some wiggly eyes to the button then hot glue to the glass or mug. Draw the spider webs and spider lets with the black sharpie marker.

Holiday Earrings

Items Needed: Holiday buttons, clip-on earrnig blanks, E6000 glue.

All it takes is a drop of glue on the erring blank and some holiday buttons. You can also use foam holiday items like the skates and Santa's hats. I found all of these at Hobby Lobby. They also sell rings to make a matching set.

Dog & Cat Christmas Trees

Items Needed: Dog or Cat buttons, miniature mug for base, modeling clay and Christmas Tree, hot glue

Put the clay in the mug so that it has enough weight to hold up the tree. Normally the trees come on some type of base. Get rid of that and put the tree in the mug. Hot glue dog or cat buttons as ornaments and whatever else you would like to have on your tree.

Button Stockings

Items Needed : Small felt stocking, buttons and hot glue

I found these stockings at Big Lots. You can make these little stocking personalized with just a few buttons.

For more cake, cupcake, treats and craft ideas and the latest books please see my blog at:

LynnDavisCakes.com

Current Books Available on Amazon.com:

Egg Crafts for All Ages

Charity Bake Sales, Fund Raiser & Ice Cream Socials

Halloween Charity Bake and Craft Sale

Getting out of the doghouse for Father's Day

Holiday, Birthday and Unique Parties

2 Hours of Babysitting and Free Cupcake Class for $15 – How I Started my Home Base Business

Sizzling Summer Recipes

Mother's Day – Gifts Made with Love

Santa Stories:
- Mrs. Claus' Cooking Class and Competition
- Earthquake at the North Pole
- Where's Molly
- Santa Paws

Life After Death – A Widow's Journey

How I Retired at Age 59

Ark Journey Series:

- The Egg Thieves
- Cretaceous Pirates
- Pirates Revenge, Stranded in the Cretaceous
- Hunting Predators

Made in the USA
Monee, IL
06 December 2022